I0102207

Stories from the

Origin

Ordinary moments in the

central desert of Australia

By

Anne Zonne Parker

Anne Z. Parker
aparker@naropa.edu
Copyright 2007
ISBN 978-0-6151-6538-7

Foreword to Stories from the Origin

Over the last century and a half there have been many hundreds of monographs and memoirs written about Australia's Aboriginal people. The most striking thing about these ethnographic studies and travelogues is that few of them have been able to get Aboriginal people right. For example, after reading more than a dozen serious studies of Aboriginal ritual life (from Durkheim to the present day), I have still to find a European researcher who can describe what sentiments Aboriginal people experience during their sacred ceremonies. The vast majority of ethnographies operate at a very great remove from the actual life lived by Australia's indigenous people. Odd as it may seem, they often appear to be disinterested in that life.

A reader can learn a great deal about Freud, gender studies, Marx, structural anthropology, or whatever has been the training and interest of the researcher or traveler, but the life-world of actual Aboriginal people will be missing. There are some exceptions, very few, but what it feels to be a traditionally oriented Aboriginal person in contemporary Australia is deeply buried beneath the mountains of paper of the published studies. What is more, I have no doubt that most of Australia's Aboriginal people prefer it that way, with their secrets left to themselves.

The present volume by Prof. Anne Zonne Parker is one of the exceptions. Unique is the most accurate way to describe this volume. It is not a "study" of Aboriginals; rather, a series of portraits of being Aboriginal are presented for the reader's consideration. Minimalist in its genre, the common European theoretical interest familiar to researchers of Aboriginal studies are set aside, and Dr. Parker aims straight for the heart of what most closely characterizes the living of indigenous Australians in their own world.

Aboriginal people will recognize themselves in these portraits. They are neither objectified nor ennobled but permitted to be who they are, in their very own ways. It may help the reader to know that for most Aboriginal people *being* is more important than *doing*, and it may be said that they are very good at it. "Good at exactly what?" the reader may want to know. Dr. Parker's portraits will provide the answer in detail, but it can be mentioned now that their expertise in *being* has to do with the close patience with which they remain attentive to the emotional states and needs of the people they are living with.

Dr. Parker once pointed out to me, more than two decades ago, that Aboriginal people keep themselves well tuned to the feelings of the people around them. It was a comment that made short shrift of a three-year study I had made of Western Desert Aboriginal people, and the comment came to serve as my compass for writing the book *Understanding Interaction in Central Australia* (Routledge 1985) based on my research.

Dr. Parker is an environmental geographer with abundant ethnographic experience. She has two master's degrees – in Central Asian Studies (Indiana University) and Geography (University of Oregon) and a PhD in Geography from Oregon. She spent a year as a Fulbright scholar living in a roadless, mountainous region of eastern Nepal studying ethnicity and agricultural practices. In addition to Ngaanyatjarra, a central Australian Aboriginal language, Dr. Parker has working knowledge of Tibetan, Nepali, and French, having lived in Tibetan monasteries, Nepali villages, and western Switzerland. She spent two years living with traditionally oriented Aboriginal people in Australia's Western Desert. She presently teaches in environmental studies at Naropa University in Boulder, Colorado.

Of course, anthropological research has proven convincingly that Aboriginal people are very good at sharing, but what they have failed to do is convey the spirit of what it is to share. By this, I mean what a person accustomed to sharing feels. Dr. Parker's book fills this void. The real people of Australia's Western Desert live and breathe on her pages. If the portraits are brief, that is because the jargon and theorizing is missing which is a situation preferable to the Aboriginal people themselves being missing. Of course, it is not an academic study, and these are only snapshots of a much greater social phenomenon that still survives. She herself has stated that it is not *her* voice that matters; instead, Dr. Parker has made the voices of Aboriginal people available to the reader who listens. The happy part is that it is not at all difficult to listen to the people who live on her pages.

Kenneth Liberman, University of Oregon
June 2004

Stories from the Origin

Table of Contents

STORIES PART 1

STORIES PART II

INTRODUCTION

Thank you for being here to read these stories.

I went to live in the Central Desert of Western Australia in 1977. There are stories from that time that have never left me. I feel inexorably called to share them. They are not my stories. They are our stories. They are asking to be told.

During the two years that we, my husband Ken and I, lived in the Central Desert I had the gift of seeing and being part of the lives of Aboriginal friends. There was nothing easy or pretty about this. There was racism, despair, alcoholism, joy, friendship, anger, boredom, and all the other things that transpire in human lives within and between cultures. But for me it was an initiation into the sacred that has never left me. These stories came like transmissions; they have not lost their power with the passing decades. They still express levels of understanding and modeling of human potential that have rarely been surpassed in my experience. The power and presence of the internal world of the Aborigines shone through the Mad Hatter's world of derelict towns, crazed mission settlements, and strange characters living out strange lives in Australia's Central Desert.

Aboriginal people are master storytellers. Their culture is the longest continuous human culture on Earth. Their stories have been told for thousands of years, perhaps 80,000 years, perhaps 100,000 as some have suggested. Consider the power of stories that old. Their stories hold the landscape and the people together. They co-create the world they live in. The stories are told at all different speeds and cadences - including repetitive chanting, or soft, sweet, low, or rhythmic sequences - depending on the purpose and texture of the story. They are told over and over again. It is in honor of the power, grace, beauty, and unimaginable wisdom of that tradition that I offer these simple stories of my own about the ordinary moments of my encounter with their lives. Here, these ordinary moments offer glimpses of sanity. By this I mean moments of great insight into the meaning of being human, moments of penetrating the modern materialistic worldview that allows a deep sanity to shine through. They are glimpses of living in the Dreamtime, glimpses of the profound meaning of being human in viable interconnection with this world.

As I sat down to write, so many stories leapt to my throat asking to be told all at once in a great shower of faith and joy. It moved me deeply just to know that they, my Aboriginal friends, exist and to know that they were still there to show that sacred origin of being human. Despite *everything*, despite the genocide and the destruction of their lives and world, they were there, fully present. I thank you, the elders I met out there, for remaining thus in timeless Dreamtime presence.

I invite you, the reader, to enter into the stories. Become the characters. Especially, take these moments into your heart.

PART ONE
Meeting the Desert

Sister, We Are So Glad You Have Come

The red earth held my attention as I walked. It was a deep, dark red that penetrated clothes and hair, so that everything -- trees, houses, and cars -- was red in some way. Old houses with a few bedraggled lawns gave way to a line of shops along a single street. It was a small town. It made no more than a dent in the vastness of that part of Western Australia. The town seemed a transitory fantasy in light of the ancient landscape that stretched for miles out to the horizon in all directions. The tiny town was a remnant of what it had once been in its heyday, when Herbert Hoover had made good in gold mining.

It was my first day in Leonora. As I made the short journey from our new home in a simple government house to the main street of Leonora, I felt the trepidation and excitement of being new among unknown people in an unknown community. I had come to work with the older Aboriginal women to record their knowledge of plants. Ken, my husband, had come to document sacred sites for the Western Australian Museum. All this we hoped might convey some of the importance of the Aboriginal understanding of the land to mainstream Australian society. I was scared to leave the familiar world where I could easily operate in my own language, and I didn't yet know what this new world would bring. But my heart was completely open.

On Main Street I surveyed the line of simple and dilapidated storefronts. I didn't really need to buy anything; I simply needed to make some contact with my new world. Shopping was part of my familiar cultural world, something I could do to recognize myself in the middle of an alien desert. There were a few cars parked along the street, but no immediate sign of activity. Many of the shops seemed to be empty or abandoned. I headed towards the first one that looked open. The white paint on the storefront was cracked and peeling. The front window display was empty; there was only a thick layer of red dust where the display items would have been.

The only thing to suggest that the store was open was a small "OPEN" sign taped on the door. Stepping in from the brilliant sunlight I was blinded for a minute as my eyes adjusted to the dark interior.

Before me lay a long thin room empty except for a large table at the far end. It was covered with notebooks, pens, and other stationery items. I immediately thought, "Oh, I'll buy a pen and use that as an excuse for a conversation." Used to being anonymous in stores in Perth or San Francisco, I suddenly grasped that in a small town every detail matters. With her back to me facing the display was an Aboriginal woman, perhaps in her forties, wearing a loose, flowered dress. She was barefoot and her soft brown hair fell to her shoulders. She was speaking with a white woman who stood behind the display facing her.

The white woman was dressed more elaborately in a blouse, mid-calf skirt, and shoes. Her hair was drawn up in a bun. The severe hairstyle mirrored the taut look of disapproval on her face as she spoke about the debt the Aboriginal woman owed. In contrast, the Aboriginal woman calmly explained her situation. The white woman was tense and judgmental, while the Aboriginal woman was patient and attentive. The Aboriginal woman turned on her heel just as I moved to a spot next to her.

As she turned she looked at my eyes. I looked directly back at hers. Nothing was spoken. I approached the dour-faced English woman. She seemed to have caught my gaze with the Aboriginal woman and carried her sour mood over to me. Taking no time to say hello, she sold me a pen. Disappointed, I left quickly, heading out into the street.

The Aboriginal woman was waiting for me. She stepped up quickly and said,

"Sister, we are so glad you have come."

"Sister, we are so glad you have come.: The acceptance and accuracy of intuition nearly knocked me off my feet. Even now, thirty years later, I can never tell this story without a catch of heart and tears coming to my eyes. I had never felt truly welcomed anywhere. Her words pinned me to the earth, filled my heart with meaning, and knocked linear time right out of my mind. With an unclogged soul she had no trouble seeing that I was there in good heart. . Despite defeat, desecration, destitution and despair, this woman wearing rags, unwashed, and with hair wild with desert dirt had internal presence as clear as light. I was home at last.

There seemed to be, in essence, three zones in Australia, three concentric circles. In the coastal zones, where most of the cities are located Aboriginal culture was nearly completely decimated through disease and destruction; there are small populations of Aboriginal

people in the cities. The next zone is the zone of agriculture and cattle stations. Here Aboriginal people are marginalized on the edge of towns in settlements or on the station lands themselves. There is a range of living conditions from old houses to encampments. Weaving in and out of this zone and the next are mines and mining towns like Leonora where whites live in small towns and Aboriginal people live near or on the edge of towns.

The final zone, the heart of Australia, and the heart of the desert, contains Aboriginal settlements, areas of land set aside like reservations for Aboriginal communities. There, although their lives do not follow their traditional nomadic patterns, they live on the land in wiltjas *(windbreaks) and have some say in the structure of their lives and communities. The history of removal of children to schools, disenfranchisement of land, intentional genocide, and even bomb testing has massively disrupted Aboriginal life and settlement patterns. But their deep relationship with land and spiritual life lives on.*

In Australia the culture gap between the intensely non-material world of Aboriginal culture and the intensely material world of the Europeans is enormous and has lent itself to huge cross-cultural misunderstanding. As an outsider stepping into this world as it was in the 1970's, when the policies of removing half-caste children from their mothers had only just ended, it was a shock to experience the historical legacy. In light of all this, it was a stunning welcome from the woman I met that day in Leonora.

Body Language

One day I was staying at home in the little white government-issue house in Leonora. Seated at my desk I slowly scanned the room. Fine red dust covered my papers, the desk, the bed, the floor, my hands and every corner of the room. Here, in the vast spaces of the Central Desert, the notion of indoor space and keeping things clean seemed patently absurd. As I scanned, my endless efforts to keep the house clean played through my mind. Eventually I left off my quiet contemplation of the room and turned back to pressing plants. I was collecting plant specimens and interviewing Aboriginal elders on their ethnobotanical understanding for my MA thesis. I carried on laying out the dried plants on mounting paper for a while, but somehow I could not quite block out the reality of the desert at hand and effectively return to "normal." Alone in the dusty room I could not get the notion of the absurdity of what I was doing out of my mind. I could not concentrate on my work.

No longer able to work I began looking out the window. There, on the unpaved road our house sat on, I saw an English woman walking by. She was short and stocky. In her tight skirt and baggy sweater she looked rather conventionally dressed. She had a dog on a leash. Snip, snap, snip, snap, she took her rigid steps in tight shoes. *She* was going to be "proper" despite that deep red timeless landscape. Snip, snap, snip, snap - an unhappy walk confined to small spaces. Her choices, like mine, in light of the desert world that held us in its thrall, too, seemed absurd. I simply sat and stared out the window at the desert after she passed.

An hour later I was still staring out the window. Along came two Aboriginal men with long, liquid gaits, as if in answer to my wordless questions about how to be at home in this landscape. Both were tall and slender with long legs. The older man's short pants and worn shirt hung easily on his long, lean frame. The younger man's torso, covered only in fine desert dust, mirrored the natural grace of the older man. Their gaits said that they had moved miles across the vast landscape, and belonged there, as did the dogs harmonizing beside them. Their feet knew the land. It was a stunning, startling contrast to the woman who had preceded them.

Body language can speak a million words. It can be seen in a split-second glance. This moment, of seeing the men glide past my window, knocked me out of my cultural vision of reality. It was the answer to my unspoken question about the land and how to be in it.

I discovered that trying to explain in words that sudden shift or awareness into seeing different realities never did much good. Friends immediately threw up walls: "But we can't go back to that time, the population is too great we couldn't all be hunters and gatherers...." and on and on. But wait, hush, don't you want to hear about the presence? Are you sure it only occurs when the outer physical circumstances are "primitive?. Don't you want to let it into your soul before you block it off with regret or disbelief? The silent instruction by those two me of relationship with the land transcended space and time.

Robert Lawlor, an author who writes passionately about th4 wisdom of Aboriginal culture in his book Stories of the First Day, tells the story of his colleague, Brian, an Aboriginal man who had tried to disown his heritage. Brian had left Australia for a while but on his return he beheld an elder standing out in the desert. One look from that elder transmitted to him the significance of his own heritage. Lawlor describes Brian's experience of that moment as follow: "While he was driving through a scorching hot desert region, his binoculars picked up a lonely figure standing like an apparition on a rocky outcrop (Brian says) 'It was the first time I had actually seen a tribal person. He was standing on one leg, with the other folded and the sole of that foot pressing against the inside of his thigh...His oiled body had the soft matte veneer of desert dust, increasing the sense that his nakedness had only recently been transformed from the earth itself... We stopped the Land River and I stared at him for a long time. His body remained motionless, as if his spine were connecting the earth to the sky. As the Aborigines would say, he was beholding his country, seeing all the stories from the Dreaming from these sacred places...After seeing that tribal person I knew I could never hide or be ashamed of my Aboriginality. From that time onward all my work, all that I learned, all my energy would go toward revealing the beauty and power of my culture.'" (Lawlor, 1991,3-4)

Fucking People Fucking Money

One day, as seen out the window, an old Aboriginal woman came. She was wearing a dress, worn simply as Aboriginal women do, just as covering with no necessity of all the values laden on it by those from whose culture the dress had come. She carried a stick, a long walking stick. She walked alone, black feet barefoot on the red sand. As she walked she chanted and beat the stick in a rhythm to her chant, "Fucking people, fucking money, fucking people, fucking money..." Over and over she chanted as she walked.

It was Saturday in Leonora. Lots of extra white people had come to town for a "footie" game. People had parked their cars on the postage stamp lawns and gone in to friends' houses to enjoy the game. It was a good time to gather to share life and news. Afterwards they celebrated with lots of beer and barbecues outside. They saw her coming. "Stupid drunk old Aboriginal woman," they said as she passed by chanting.

Was she merely a poor, deranged old woman wandering like a misfit in a modern world? Or was she something more, perhaps a sane voice to be heard at last when ears and hearts could hear? It is traditional for older Aboriginal women to take up a stick *when things are out of balance* and walk through camp chanting and stamping the stick with a rhythmic beat. A way of ritualized and accepted "madness" in which frustrations and concerns can be expressed and *heard.* " My son-in-law is beating my daughter!" perhaps, or whatever concerns she might have that she could chant. Everyone would listen and would try to pull back on their behavior. It was a time to learn how one's behavior affected others.

So she was chanting for that place, for the loss of the people's soul in materialism, for money as measure of human value. Not a meaningless chant and a chant that in the end could not be avoided.

.

She Doesn't Speak Her Language

In search of the people who had once lived in an area to the north, we went to a station to interview an old woman. She was said to be the very last member of her tribe. As we drove up to the small, collapsing station house an old bitter white man came out. He couldn't understand why we had come to talk to the old woman and not to him.

He lived alone in the station: his wife had died. He was bitter, angry, and lonely. The old Aboriginal woman lived in a tiny *wiltja*, small like a dog house, outside. They had known each other for years. She had cooked his meals and washed his clothes. No doubt he had slept with her. He spoke about her disparagingly. "Oh, she doesn't know her language." With much effort we finally got past him to talk to her.

Ken addressed her in Ngaanyaatjarra. She spoke back. The old man got irritated since he couldn't understand or manipulate the interaction. He stomped off to the house. She told stories about the land, the plants, and her people. She told how her mother had tried to hide her to keep her from being taken by the whites. Her mother had used the powder of burned sandalwood seeds to make her skin look darker, so they wouldn't want to take her. At last, however, she had had to enter the white world since there were so few of them left. And there she was, after all those years, living with quiet grace, while the man who "owned" her people's land lived in empty bitterness.

The quality of bitterness in many of the white people I met out there really struck me. When I arrived I naturally turned to them as allies or possible friends since we shared, it seemed, some aspect of larger cultural reality. Indeed, I did make some wonderful friends. But many of the white people we met were so walled in with bitterness and alienation that it was hard to connect. Their discontent could have arisen in fighting with a land and landscape that would never fit with their cultural training, or the confusion and even fear in interacting across the great cultural divide. It is hard to say. The tendency to anger, despair, and even madness of whites "out there" really stood out. Of course there were some white people who loved that land and felt deeply at home in their own way. I had not set out to be critical of European culture. It was as if that worldview was so alien to the land out there in the desert that it seemed to have held its own trial and hung itself. Somehow, in following its own logic, it had created an empty sort of mad and bitter world.

Then there is the question of who is critiquing whom. I can make no claim to special status in the meeting of culture worlds and the creation or recreation of oppressive circumstances:

"In any treatment of colonialism, racism and the discourses associated with these, the question of voice becomes crucial. Is it enough for example, to hear only about and only from the colonizers, and from the critics that, inevitably, eventually emerge from among the descendants of those communities wherein the colonizing effort first began? More crudely, can we be

satisfied with hearing white folks commenting critically on white folks, and will such texts yield enough knowledge from or about the colonized themselves? Will such texts occlude those very voices, spaces, and meaning systems that they ostensibly set out to remind us have been occluded? These are the challenges that for many years have faced the critics of colonial and racist discourses. On the other hand, what does it mean when white scholars draw upon the voices of the colonialized within their own texts? What kinds of power relations are reinstated then? Further, what claims about authenticity, purity and restored originality might appropriately or erroneously be made, in those moments when the white historian, ethnographer or cultural critic seeks to draw into her text indigenous, colonized and/or 'subaltern' voices in order to document that which has been 'lost'?" (Cowlishaw 1999 xi-xii)

There is no escape from the complexity of the relationships here. I certainly make no claim to expertise about Aboriginal reality. As the voice of a visiting white woman, I am sharing my perception. For me the ordinary moments are worth recording. These moments stand as doorways opening not away from the complexity but into the complexity. These doorways are glimpses of sanity into the meaning of being human.

There are many Aboriginal languages. In the Western Desert area where Leonora is located. One of the major languages is Ngaanyatjarra. This area had been home to many groups, who circulated through it in nomadic fashion with the seasons.

"Traditional Aboriginal people were multi-lingual and it would seem that there were originally around 300,

and possibly up to 500, Aboriginal languages and some 600-700 dialects, all of which appear to be generically related. It is of great concern today that many Aboriginal languages face the threat of extinction. At a rough estimate, only 10 percent of Aboriginal people still speak their indigenous languages, and of the original 270 or so distinct languages, two thirds (about 160) are either extinct or have only a handful of elderly speakers remaining. Only about twenty of the surviving languages are actively transmitted to children and adults." (Voight and Drury 1998, 12)

Invisible worlds

So many times there were stories of two worlds living side by side in ignorance. Driving up to a big, well-run station one day, Ken and I told the muscular, hard-working young white station owner that we had come to meet some of the Aboriginal men who lived and worked there. We planned to take two of them out to survey a sacred site. He said that the men on his station didn't even know the names of the hills nearby, so they wouldn't be much good.

As we stood there by the stockyard facing the young station owner, several old Aboriginal men came up and stood slightly behind him. They mumbled a few words."Yes boss, oh yeah, we don't know much." The station owner did not turn to look at them and continued to address us. However, the men behind him were silently addressing us too. With their hands they carried out an elaborate conversation with the Aboriginal elder who had accompanied us. Their hands said, "When this is over come on around the back and we can make all the necessary arrangements." I was amazed at this display of invisible worlds. I thought, " If you do not honor people you cannot see them."

When asked the names of nearby hills or landscape features, Aboriginal people cannot give the sacred name so they say something in their language like "Oh that," or "That over there." So many of the Aboriginal words for landscape features used by English speakers features are just like that. These strange names appear on maps. What an irony when every hill is held in loving detail in story, song, and clear geographic memory in the Dreamtime.

If we don't honor each other we cannot see each other.
If we don't honor the land we cannot see it either.
If we honor each other we can see each other.
If we honor the land we can see her.

As I experienced it, Aboriginal people are able to speak in three languages simultaneously. One is the normal verbal exchange we consider to be language. The second is an elaborate series of hand gestures. This does not seem to be a symbolic language like signing that has to be learned and cannot be understood by those who have not studied it. It is an elaborate use of the hands to show actions, shapes, sizes, and textures of things and some of it is immediately understandable without training. Other components of it would require practice and training in the meanings of certain gestures. In short, it feels more accessible than current traditions of signing used by the deaf. The third language could be described as the language of empathy, paying close attention to the feeling quality of interpersonal communication in such a way that much is communicated without words. They, at least the elders, are so skillful that it too is very accessible to those of us from other cultures. In a later story "Pouring Water into Water," this is demonstrated by my mother arriving from suburbia in the USA and spontaneously being able to feel a real depth in communication even without words. This sounds like a fantasy, but you simply have to see it to realize this is more than within the range of normal human capacity. We have trained ourselves out of it, but we can recognize and name it when we experience someone who has grown up with it as a normally developed capacity.

Houses and Tea: doing other realities

Lorraine, my neighbor in Leonora, was a middle-aged Aboriginal woman working as a cook at a government home for kids without families. She was of indistinguishable age, perhaps in her late thirties. She was kind, and she was tired. She lived in the house behind ours with four or five kids whom she looked after by herself. She was a woman of courage, a woman struggling to survive between two worlds. Her situation was further complicated by an abusive husband who, as well, was part of the struggle between two worlds.

I liked to visit Lorraine's house. I loved houses that were empty except for the people and love and an essential bed or two.   Lorraine's house was like that. I could go there when I was lonely to find company and conversation. We would all sit on the floor or eat whatever was in the kitchen. I always felt welcome.

And Lorraine could escape the abuse at home with a restoring visit to my place. She would come bringing one little boy or girl. I would serve tea and we would talk together as the child ran around on a rampage attacking every material value I ever held. The little child couldn't believe that I stored food for more than one day and wanted to eat it immediately. He or she attacked the objects on my desk. I would sit poised between wanting my welcome to be as warm as theirs and trying to explain how or why one shouldn't touch this or that. It was an intense spot to sit in. Lorraine would quietly track the child's progress around the house, noting what she was up to, but not stopping her. Nothing in my house was left untouched except for two things.

There were two things that Lorraine watched carefully and which she guarded. One was the old grinding stone from the desert that Ken had brought back. It sat on the counter in the kitchen where we used it to crush buckwheat for chapattis. It was a sacred stone and the child was prevented from touching it. The other sacred thing was the entirely empty room that we used for meditation. Without ever asking what they did in that room, Lorraine would not let the child even enter it. All this played out before my eyes as a direct display of *doing different realities*. It set into perspective all the material values and choices we had made and balanced them before the invisible yet powerful realm of the other values.

Lorraine would come over and, reading all my foot prints in the earth around the house, know exactly what I had been doing all day: "Oh, I see you went out and came back with something heavy." Indeed I had gone out to gather wood for the little hot water heater. Or she would come to chat with Ken when he returned radiant and joyful from his work with the old men. Taking a swipe with her finger at the dust on the four-wheel drive she would say, "Oh, I see you've been out Wiluna way and up to Warburton," accurately reading the layers of dust accumulated. These were not superhuman or mystical skills. They were the learned skills of one who lived in the natural world.

Indeed the whole notion of houses was strange. In traditional desert culture a house should be burned when someone dies. But that did not jive well with the more permanent notion of house that was present in European culture. Our Aboriginal neighbors a few blocks away demonstrated this with their style of living. An elderly couple had been given a house as a kind and charitable act. They liked it and used it according to their perception of it. They camped outside it on whichever side was appropriate given the wind. It was an excellent windbreak in which they could store some food or "things." It also served as an excellent source of firewood. Why live inside it where you couldn't see your friends coming, or feel the wind or enjoy the sun? This outraged the neighbors, needless to say.

The meeting of material values and non-material values creates a huge disaster of non-communication of human dignity across cultures in Australia as it has other places in the world. To my mind the gradient was perhaps the most extreme here in a culture with almost no material objects. The initial fate of the arriving Europeans was to completely miss the depth of wisdom and understanding of Aboriginal culture. They saw things only as "primitive" and needing improvement.

I forgot to clean my mind

Each morning in the little white house in Leonora I tried to clear my mind with meditation, as much as I could. I would go to the little back porch room that we had made a meditation place and sit for an hour. There was nothing in that room. Then I would go on with the rest of the day. Some days I felt good, other days I was bored or distracted. So it went with working with the mind. This all seemed to be a personal work, something important, but perhaps not visible in the world around me.

One morning I was in a "hurry," anxious to collect more "data." After all, I did have a research grant from the Institute of Aboriginal Studies and I was doing a Master's degree through Murdoch University. In light of this state of mind, that day I decided I was too busy to meditate. I had to hurry to meet the women who had agreed to go out looking at plants with me. I hurried out across the red earth to Lorraine's house where I was to meet Lorraine and the old woman.

As I walked up I could sense them sensing me. "Oh god," I thought, "I forgot to clean my mind." It was like standing before an audience on stage and suddenly realizing there was split pea soup all down my shirt. Not mesmerized by material things they could "see" my mental state clearly. It was not a paranormal skill, something strange, but a harmonized sense of perception that was naturally part of their way of seeing. No words were necessary.

I sat down and tried to calm my mind and "be" with them, not focusing on taking. There was only a seeing on their part, not judgment of me. I turned my eyes to the earth to ground myself, as I sat next to them. They patiently and silently waited until my task was complete. I felt much better. Not a word had been spoken, but it was more clear than any verbal advice I have ever been given.

Later we went out on a picnic and talked for a long time about the textures and colors of the plants around a dried pool that sometimes filled in the rain. I was learning about plants, but it didn't "stick" in my mind because it was accumulated knowledge, not the voices of the plants themselves or the years of experience living with and from them. Textures and colors, however, I didn't forget. Lorraine cooked meat for the picnic, simply setting it directly on the coals. Centuries of tools and objects dropped from my mind as I saw that.

I had known from the look into the woman's eyes in the shop that first day in town, that *there was no linear progression of history*. Material history, yes, but internal history, any kind of primitive mind improved on or surpassed in the spiritual realm by the modern material world, no.

In their laughter

Once we went to visit three old ladies who lived far to the west. We drove for hours across the vast, flat, red landscape. At last we saw them simply standing next to their *wiltjas* – wind breaks – with not a tree or a bush in sight anywhere for miles. To my eye it was a stark, empty scene. Nothing but the three old ladies and the three windbreaks. These creations rose only chest high on a standing adult. The *wiltjas* were wild, rococo constructions with an array of strange metal objects decorating them. Nothing in *Alice in Wonderland* would have seemed too strange in light of these fanciful constructions. Built of strange curls of metal, bottle tops, pieces of wood, they were little works of art.

These three women, who lived in this vast extent of empty space in their *wiltjas*, were the last members of their tribe, the only ones who knew their stories and their language. As we spoke to them the stories began to flow. For hours they described animals, plants, and seasonal migration cycles through the land that their tribe had followed. What had seemed like empty space around us filled with stories, meetings, beauty, and human details. They held stories of a whole lifetime in that place. From what had appeared to our eyes as nothing - a desolate landscape -came story after story. They remembered all that had transpired there with loving detail.

They were joyous and light and a pleasure to spend an afternoon with. The afternoon drew to a close as the sun neared the horizon and we began to think of leaving.

Finally, we asked the last question, wanting to know the answer but reluctant to ask it. "So how does it feel to be the last of your people?"

After a split second they all three burst into laughter, a joyous laughter that rang with clarity - a clarity that emptied the heart of all fixation. This from women whose people had been decimated, who had been treated like servants on land that was their birthright. In their laughter I heard the ring of understanding of the profound nature of reality; there was no mistaking it.

Their laugher penetrated the three worlds.
(Past, present, and future)

Dignity

Hidden, undestroyed, lies the Dreamtime presence.

Peter and Daisy lived out of town on land that had become someone else's "private property." This was the plight of Aboriginal people living on their traditional lands in the places where stations were established.

The day I drove out to visit them, I followed my instructions to avoid the big house and turn off at the gate that led to their camp. As I slowed down to open the gate the woman from the station saw me. Thinking I was a health worker, her eyes lit up with a pleasant hello. Then, as she saw who I was, although I had never met her, her eyes narrowed. "This is our sacred land," she said, "You can't trespass here."

"I have come to visit Peter and Daisy. They have invited me here. They do live here, don't they?" With that she begrudgingly recognized that she could not prevent me from going to where they lived even if it was "her property." She huffed off as I slid the lock on the gate and drove through. There I found Peter and Daisy sitting on the red earth near small *wiltjas*. In their camp everyone had *wiltjas*. They were was enough to provide a little shade in the day, a little shelter at night while everyone huddled around to drink tea from a Billy can (with too much sugar, handfuls) and bread from the frying pan.

Peter and Daisy were 70 years old or more I think. He was tall and distinguished, she tiny as a bird. Both of them had hair as white as snow. They had a radiant light around their eyes that one can see endlessly carved in rock carvings in northern Western Australia, something like a halo of light around the eyes. There was no other way to explain the radiance on their faces. I always felt comfortable with them. I mentally adopted them as additional grandparents. In fact they reminded me very much of my own grandparents, Pappy and Grace.

They were so gentle with their hearts and hands. They used their hands to describe the plants that day. A name of a plant would be spoken while the hands demonstrated how tall it grew, how its roots were shaped, how it was used, all without words. We walked only a short distance, but we spent hours before returning to camp. It was pleasant then just to sit and hear the stories, voiced and unvoiced. When the land and heart are full of stories and good company, there is less loneliness. I returned to visit often.

One day Peter told his story. Oh, I would have been so bitter with a story like that, but he was light. The radiance around his eyes spoke of a dignity far beyond the story he told. He was from far north, near Darwin. As a young boy he had been taken from his family to a white school (to be "whiteified"). And he had run away. A trooper was sent after him, but he had hid in a bush. Somehow the trouper had gotten off his horse to look in that bush, and Peter jumped on the horse and fled south.

He had met a man herding sheep down toward central Western Australia. He had joined up to work, only to be treated like a slave. He said it was nasty, but preferable to being in the school. The white man gave them food, dropping it over his shoulder rather than giving it directly to them as a sign of their lower status in his mind. On their long journey down to central Western Australia, he killed one of the other Aboriginal boys for not waking up on time. Peter and the other Aboriginal boys on that run finally turned in that white man for the murder when they got down to Kalgoorlie.

Peter never went back north. He stayed down in central Western Australia working on stations. He tried to get into the army for World War I, but they wouldn't let him go. He was sent to work in the forests of southwestern Australia. He described walking back out to the desert after the War. Everywhere he stopped he was treated like scum. He came to one station and asked if he could work for food. They sent him around the back to find a dirty tin can from the garbage heap to eat from and treated him like a dog; he left as soon as he could. There was no place to be treated differently at that time.

 Meanwhile, his wife Daisy had been raped by the station owner and her half-caste child had been taken off to a school in Perth to be "whiteified." (She became a capable and angry political radical when she finally finished that school). His voice spoke with dignity and calm, but at the same time seemed to ask gently, "How could people treat one another like that?" I could not offer any answer. In listening to him I could hear and feel that he had not internalized any view of himself as less. That was his awesome accomplishment. In light of the mistreatment and conscious genocide that he and his people had endured, it spoke of his deep, incorruptible spiritual presence in this world.

He and Daisy sat with timeless dignity there on the earth where her people had lived for thousands of years. Their dignity outlasted the destruction, the private property, and the madness of the modern world. They had the radiant light of elders not because of anything given or taken, but because they rest in the "Law," as Peter called it -- the Dreamtime.

Peter and Daisy's stories capture the history of their times. The legislated removal of half and often full caste Aboriginal children to school for education as menial servants persisted from the 1800s to 1970. This legacy of attempted cultural disruption was present throughout Australia at the time I arrived in 1976. There were mothers who had never seen their children again and children who had never found their parents. It is important to remember that Aboriginal residents of Australia did not receive full legal status as Australian citizens until 1967.

So the Dreamtime. I have let you feel the presence of the dreamtime in the moment-to-moment manifestation of its presence in these stories of ordinary lives. This is how I came to sense it. Reading about it and giving it language is helpful, but it is the lived quality and the indestructible presence in their lives that speaks about it best.

The Dreamtime, Tjukurrpa, is nearly impossible to explain in English. I feel that it is the description of how spirit comes into form and how material form comes into being. The Dreamtime stories "are describing *how tangible 'realities' emerged from formlessness and chaos, and how things of great beauty and worth came into the World. These stories deal with ultimate meaning and strike at the very fabric of our existence"* ... " *The Dreamtime encodes the exploits of the Spirit Ancestors, while located in the Creation of the past, and is also embodied in the present – in the land and in the Aboriginal descendents of those original beings. In this way, the Dreamtime encompasses past reality and future possibilities in an eternally sacred present. Thus all of creation and all time are contained in a diverse multiplicity of one sacred reality. Irrespective of the particular names ascribed to it, the Dreamtime holds the idea that all aspects of life are eternally interconnected in a vast web of relationship, for all creatures and all things have their sacred origin in the sacred events of Creation." (Voight and Drury 1998, 24-27)*

Many definitions have been given for the Dreamtime. This is the word that has been used in English, but it is said to not be a word really suitable for its purpose.

"Some Aboriginal people do use the phrases 'Dreamtime' and 'Dreaming' when attempting to communicate their concepts in English, but there is a certain awkwardness to these terms. The Arrente term altjianga ngambaka has the inference of 'having originated out of one's own eternity', 'immortal', 'uncreated', and it is this which is essential to the concept of 'Dreamtime' or 'Dreaming'. At the same time, altji rarma means 'to see or dream eternal things', or 'to see with eternal vision'....Some Westerners could mistakenly assume that for Aboriginal peoples the Dreamtime has the same relationship to the everyday world that dreams do in relations to our conscious waking perception – namely that one realm is a world of 'fantasy' imagery, while the other is grounded in material 'reality'. This type of definition is clearly not applicable if we are to appreciate the underlying concepts of the Aboriginal spiritual tradition, although it is certainly true in Aboriginal culture that through dreams and visions individuals may make contact with the Spirit Ancestors and in this way receive sacred information" (Voight and Drury 1998, 32)

The names for Dreamtime in Aboriginal languages are many: Tjukurpa (Pitjantjatjara of north-west South Australia); Altjeringa and related terms (Arrente of Central Australia); Wonjar or Wangarr (Yolnga of northeastern Arnhem Land); Ngarangkarni (Kukatja of Western Australia); Lalai (Ngarinyin of Kimberly region of Western Australia). It is said to mean something more like the quintessence of existence itself, which includes or encompasses the land and people.

"Unlike other religious traditions which celebrate at separate times to everyday life a revelatory event in the long past, the Dreamtime of Aboriginal practice is celebrated and lives in whatever exists and transpires in the present – in all aspects of Creation in an eternal now. In this sense all time exists in the present moment and all life – the Spirit Ancestors, the Earth, the Cosmos and all species – are aspects of the inherited divine order and thus are sacramental. There is no 'thing' in Aboriginal consciousness that is 'nothing'. There is no aspect, no creature –be it a dung beetle, a poisonous snake or a human being – that does not have its place and its role to play in the ordained sacred pattern of Creation. There are no gods, no religious hierarchies, no segregation of 'good' and 'bad', no unsavory bits, and no separation between the physical and the spiritual or nature, humanity and culture. All came into being at the one time, and all of these dimensions are reflections of each other." (Voight and Drury 1998, 26-27)

The Dreamtime is something that took place around the time just before one's grandparents, when everything was created. While it is "long ago" it is also a sense of history that is much more recent (even contemporary) than anything Western. In this way the Dreamtime stories exist in the ancient past and the active present simultaneously. The Dreamtime encompasses past and future simultaneously in an eternally sacred present and "all aspects of life are eternally interconnected in a vase web of relationship, for all creatures and all things have their origin in the sacred events of Creation". (Voight and Drury 1998, 27)

For me it was the fact that Peter and Daisy were "resting in the Dreamtime" despite what had happened to them that deeply affected me. They knew that they had their place and role to play in the ordained sacred pattern of Creation. The center of their being rested in this great reality that held their life in a dignity well beyond the treatment they had experienced. They had not so much followed a spiritual path as stayed within an unshakable sense of human place and belonging in the universe.

Maps

One day in March we went out to document a sacred site with Peter and Snowy Hill. We drove out of Leonora heading east. We picked them up at the nearby station where they lived with Daisy and other family members. Snowy was the Dreamtime keeper of the site we were going to visit. It was contentious because a mining company was saying there was nothing sacred there, no important site, no stone carvings, nothing. We were going to hear Snowy's stories about his place.

On the flat and almost featureless landscape we drove on east, then north, then west. We stopped when the car could no longer navigate the terrain. Snowy led the way, walking south along a canyon. He was the Dreamtime keeper so he would guide us. We walked in low hills going south, a little east, and further south. We arrived at the place where patterns of hands and feet and animal tracks were traced like petroglyphs in the stone. It was good to be out there in the bright sun – no roads, just the elegance of the low desert hills and birdcalls surrounding us. We sat there running our hands gently over the patterns carved in the rocks. We felt honored to be shown the ancient place and told the stories here. The local whites told their member of state parliament that the Aboriginals had made the whole thing up (including the ancient carvings), and that they were put up to it by two American radicals (I and my husband).

While we were contemplating the site, quietly and curiously, Peter looked directly at me and asked me, "Which way is Leonora?" I sensed from his glance at Snowy that this was not a casual question. They liked me. They wanted to know how much I had understood about their land.

I focused on my mental map of the land and where we had driven and walked, slowly visualizing it all. Then I pointed. They burst into grins! I was not far off. She was not bad, they thought! For them, who never wave a hand in a random gesture, every direction, every hand gesture was accurate by dead reckoning even if many hundreds of miles away. They had internal maps of fabulous accuracy enlivened by mythic stories. The mind thinks best in stories and myths -- what better way to imbed knowledge?

Reckoning. The singing geography of the landscape is everywhere evident in Aboriginal perception, in the memorizing of geometric patterns on sacred boards and sacred bodies and the chanting of the stories expressed in the lines of Dreamtime beings that had crisscrossed that landscape. The result is an incredibly accurate inner and outer map of the real world.

The Song lines are part of the fabric of the universe I think. Ley lines, Feng shui lines, energy lines; we have heard of them. They have been felt or understood in most cultures in some form, some language. In Australia they have not been forgotten. They have been remembered for perhaps 80,000 years.

The Song lines are lines given voice in the stories and songs that cross the landscape in Australia:
"He went on to explain how each totemic ancestor, while traveling through the country, was thought to have scattered a trail or words and musical notes along the

line of his footprints, and how these Dreaming tracks lay over the land as the 'ways' of communication between the most far-flung tribes, 'A song,' he said, 'was both the map and the direction finder. Providing you knew the song, you could always find your way across the country.'

In theory, at least, the whole of Australia could be read as a musical score. There is hardly a rock or creek in the country that could not or had not been sung about. One could visualize the Song lines as spaghetti of Iliads and Odysseys writhing this way and that, in which every 'episode' was readable in terms of geology.

'By episode," I asked, 'you mean "sacred site"?'

'I do.' (Chatwin 1987, 13)

This is not an old idea, something nearly forgotten. The Song lines are alive both on the land and in the heart/mind of Aboriginal people. I think of it as the singing geography of the landscape. Memorizing geometric patterns on sacred boards, chanting the stories of Dreamtime beings that had crisscrossed that landscape allows this tradition to live. This does many things at once: it connects each person with the land and their responsibility to it; it keeps the story life in the community alive; it allows people to find resources and retain an orientation in a vast landscape; and it continually sings the landscape into being.

When he drove them out into the desert, Ken directly observed old men who, through singing in their heads, could identify every landscape feature and edible resource 300 miles from where they had ever been.

"It was one thing to persuade a surveyor that a heap of boulders were the eggs of the Rainbow Snake, or a lump of reddish sandstone was the liver of a speared kangaroo. It was something else to convince him that a featureless stretch of gravel was the musical equivalent of Opus 111.

By singing the world into existence, he said, the Ancestors had been poets in the original sense of poesis, meaning 'creation.' No Aboriginal could conceive that the created world was in any way imperfect. His religious life had a single aim: to keep the land the way it was and should be. The man who went "Walkabout" was making a ritual journey. He trod in the footprints of his Ancestors. He sang the Ancestor's stanzas without changing a world or a note – and so recreated the Creation.

'Sometimes,' said Arkady, 'I'll be driving my "old men" through the desert, and we'll come to a ridge of sandhills and suddenly they'll start singing. "What are you singing?" I'll ask, and they'll say, "Singing up the country, boss. Makes the country come quicker".
'

Aboriginals could not believe the country existed until they could see it and sing it – just as, in the Dreamtime, the country had not existed until the Ancestors sang it.

'So the land", I said, 'must first exist as a concept in the mind? Then it must be sung? Only then can it exist?
'

'True'
'In otherworlds, "to exist" is "to be perceived"?'

'Yes.'

'Sounds suspiciously like Bishop Berkeley's Refutation of Matter.'

'Or Pure Mind Buddhism,' said Arkady, 'which also sees the world as illusion.'"
(Chatwin 1987, 14)

People hold the song of the place where they were born. They are the ones who keep that place alive in ritual and song. They are responsible for the well-being of that place. Everyone's presence here in the world has wonderful meaning and purpose. Each voice is of value for the creation of the world.

Do you see how strange it is to not remember the song lines?

We Weep Together

One day I was waiting for the men to do something, that as a woman I could not participate in. What this meant was time alone in the desert to simply sit and think. I was sitting on the hot red sand in a small swale surrounded by *spinifex* clumps and a few *mulga* bushes.

From somewhere nearby an Aboriginal woman appeared and came to sit beside me. I had not seen her or known there was another person around. She sat close. The deep incense of wood smoke permeated her clothes and hair. She was just a little bit drunk. The smell of wine mingled with the smoke and sweat. The wine made her more outgoing, I expect, than usual. The urgency in her manner was real. She needed to communicate something.

We began a clumsy conversation with my broken Ngaanyaatjarra and her broken English. At first it was not at all clear that we were communicating anything. Amid the jumble of broken language and confusion I felt awkward and anxious. What was she trying to ask me? Was she too drunk for a coherent conversation? She leaned toward me, intent on communicating. She seemed to be talking, waving her arms, and drawing in the sand all at once. None of it made sense.

I stopped looking at her face and began to look at her hands. Then it dawned on me what she was doing. She was drawing over and over again the symbolic pattern of her Dreamtime place, her sacred place, with geometrical patterns in the red earth as she talked. Three parallel lines, a circle, a ridge of earth, her hands moving like someone signing in sign language, hands sure that I would know what she meant. She was urgently and frantically signing the symbol of the place for which she is the guardian keeper. It was a hand map. She was speaking earth language. My heart rushed open and then I could hear her words.

"My place is being destroyed, we can no longer go there..." I heard the words and then I could feel her deep, deep anguish, like the cry of the earth itself. She was crying for her sacred place. My heart wanted to cry too. I could feel the pent up grief rising to the surface.

She saw that she had communicated. We simply sat and wept together.

A Sacred Place

The long journeys were with the men. We would set off in the government vehicle that Ken had for his job. Food, tools, and water all placed in the Jeep, we were soon covered in deep red dust as we drove on and on through the desert. Suddenly there would be a man sitting by an old windmill, nothing else in sight. He was waiting at the appointed spot to meet us. He would come wearing only his clothes, with tobacco and matches. That was it for luggage.

Off to camp on red earth by fires. Ken and I slept in sleeping bags, but the men slept next to the fire, burning logs all night. We shared everything including flat tires popped on *mulga* stakes, canned peaches with canned cream, and red dust everywhere. We traveled together through the great spaces, the beautiful red rocks, and the ghost gums. Circumambulations in timeless red space. Sacred space.

It was truly sacred space. There was one old Aboriginal man who was the Dreamtime keeper of a sacred water hole. It was being polluted and eroded by countless cattle. When asked if his sacred water hole should be protected from the ravages of grazing cattle by the construction of a fence, he answered, "It is a sacred place, all living things should come."

I began to see that the white man had conquered not so much because of superior moral or physical force, but because of the destructive qualities of a materialistic worldview and a self-centered insulation from this more sensitive vision of things. To suggest this is not, I feel, idealizing things, but simply stating the circumstances.

Real Love

An image of the Western Desert stuck in my mind before I headed back to Perth and thence to Nepal that winter. Ken had to take several old men out in the desert for a day. I was left with two women sitting on the ground far north of Lenora. I was seated cross-legged on the ground facing the two young Aboriginal women. Behind me was a black tent of some kind. In front of me was a vast sea of broken glass and strange bits of rusted metal objects.

The two young women sat cross-legged playing with a baby boy of perhaps two years. He wore nothing; his little tummy was plump. His body was streaked with dirt and sweat. His hair was blonde, like many young Aboriginal children, matted with dirt and standing straight on end. I wanted to not hold back any of my essential human feeling because of being blocked by the material circumstances surrounding the child. Slowly, as I sat struggling to be present, I began to realize that his rounded body and plump little stretched out arms combined with his wild hair on end and the halo of light around him reflecting off the broken glass, looked for all the world like a tiny, living version of Vajrapani. A wrathful image from Tibetan Buddhist iconography, Vajrapani, is a symbol of the energy of wisdom, depicted surrounded by a halo of wisdom energy flames.

There, I thought, I had somewhat laboriously clarified my mental image from perceiving suffering to perceiving spiritual presence. With this transposed image, I could remember the pure essence of the little being before me. Feeling a little pleased with my efforts, I turned to look back at the young woman who was his mother. In her eyes I saw complete and total love for that child. No translation was necessary. I sucked in my breath recognizing the difference between my theoretical efforts and the real thing.

PART TWO
Return to the Desert

She burns her thesis

Back in Leonora, there was a very frail old woman who came with me to speak about the plants. She couldn't move much. I had to lift her gently into my truck to take her from her camp out into the bush. One day as we sat on the shore of a salt-encrusted dry lakebed she simply asked me, "How can you just study our knowledge of plants when we are dying? What use is that knowledge without us?" That question sank deep to the bone.

The faces of my academic advisors were far away in strange buildings on the edge of a vast continent. They seemed to have nothing to do with reality here. One of my advisors, Geoffrey, had charmed my mother when she was visiting with tales of morning mists at Cambridge (or was it Oxford)? That all was too far away to hold me as a myth. This strange dry gathering of things I was engaged in seemed purposeless. I just sat there on the salt with that question burning in my heart.

Shortly after that we moved out to Docker River in the Northern Territory, the very "Centre" of Australia. There I would be working for the moment-to-moment welfare of the community. I began to envision destroying my thesis. I sent some good plant specimens to a few really sweet botanists I knew. After all, they loved the plants, and no one had named them yet in the conventional terms of European science. The Aboriginal friends I spoke with had many names for all of them. They had some language of hand gestures for them too. They

One night as the sun was setting golden and purple over the Peterman Range, I found a 50-gallon drum. I placed my year and a half of research, plant samples, and notes in the drum. I lit it on fire and watched the glow of the flames rise up and then die down as the night deepened. When it was all gone, I returned to our trailer to sit quietly and meditate. I knew my people, other white people, would think I was crazy, giving up the power and possibility such work would have brought me in my world. Later they would look apologetically away when I said I had burned my thesis. Poor dear, they thought, she couldn't retain a grip on reality. But what "reality" was I gripping?

Shabbat Shalom

The day the Queen's Representative came to Docker River was an unforgettable day. We should have trained everyone to do dances and served tea and done all the correct things, but we did not.

The men of the council decided that the three eldest elders representing the three principal dialect groups should greet him as he arrived from his plane. All the community would gather to greet him at the airfield. Then we would bring him to the settlement where he and everyone else would sit on the ground to discuss real matters. He was the Australian Head of State coming to find out for himself what traditionally oriented Aboriginal people were like. It was to be an important day.

My task was to stay in the office so I could answer all incoming radio calls, so I heard all about this later. What they said was that the three elders decided to have a shower and wear new clothes. They decided this rather at the last minute; in fact the decision was taken only when they heard the plane overhead. They had never used a shower before so it got very complicated and began to take a very long time. Meanwhile the Queen's Representative's plane landed. All of the men present began to go into a huge quandary. Who could greet this great man since the elders were not yet there? It was entirely inappropriate for a young person to do it, and those close to being elders would not step forward because they didn't want to act as if they were arrogant. The Governor-General got out of the plane and stood before a totally silent crowd of people. No one dared to step forward. At last some of the men grabbed Ken by the arms. He was reluctant since he wanted the

Governor-General to face Aboriginal people without mediation, so he had worn old clothes to reduce the likelihood of his playing a formal role. They thrust him forward, saying that only he could do it without repercussions.

So, dressed in the oldest blue jeans in his possession, Ken reluctantly stepped forward, smiling and extending his hand. Seeing that the Governor-General was clearly Jewish, as was Ken, and that it was the Sabbath, he simply said "Shabbat Shalom." The Northern Territory government's representative on the occasion was clearly irritated with this unkempt young American (and unaccustomed to Jewish ironic humor) and began to protest. The Governor-General motioned him to be quiet and replied without a hitch, "Shabbat Shalom". Later, other white folks would say of Ken that he had been too forward, putting himself out there when it should have been the elders, but that was not the story.

The three elder elders did finally show up, much later, looking clean with new clothes, not at all concerned that their idea of time had been different. The dignitaries accompanying the Governor-General could not believe that we had no children dancing, etc., and that we simply asked him to sit on the plain ground and talk plainly. We thought the ground can educate people, especially the Governor-General. One of them whipped out a pink cushion cover edged with lace for him to sit on the ground. He himself didn't seem to mind.

The events of the day went on, but I was alone in the Quonset hut. Late in the afternoon one of the elders, a gentle man from the Pitanjarra tribe came into the office. He looked at me quietly. He held the corner of a piece of paper in his hand. He gave it to me silently as if to say "you keep it." It was the title to all the land they had always lived on all these centuries and millennia. That was the historically momentous event for which the Governor-General had come that day. In this elder's gentle, but honest and wordless gesture to me, that small piece of paper took on its true significance. It was indeed only a small piece of paper as compared to the size, depth, and time of the land on which we stood.

But I thought that I should keep it so that the white people would remember this. I put it in the safe.

Docker River was way out beyond Uluru (Ayers Rock). As a sedentary camp in what had been a nomadic world it was, like all things out there, a strange meeting of cultures. There were Ngaanyatjarra and Pitanjarra folks and a small number of Pintubi. People stayed and went, but for many it seemed to be home for now. There were clusters of wiltjas and fires. Nothing was private, everything shared.

Docker itself was pretty with red hills behind the settlement and there was just the beauty of the land in all directions. There was a little airstrip, the store, the Quonset hut office, and not much more besides the trailer homes for the staff. People out there were lucky in a way. No one owned their land, it was a reserve. There were inroads and onslaughts over time by mining companies, British bomb testing, and who knows what, but for the moment it was protected, far from the despair of the cities and mining towns.

Docker had clear, cool, pure water – a real luxury way out there in the desert. It was a refuge for Aboriginal people where a middle-aged Aboriginal who spoke English, but refused to ever speak it, could find a feeling of home. The old folks there still went walkabout and the ceremonies still took place. The land was beautiful, filled with flowers in the spring rains, and ungrazed by cattle. It had the feeling of being one of those places in the world where the balance of nature was still felt. It was still mostly their world.

Tjupurrula Comes Unclothed

Tjupurrula was the spokesperson for the people who had come from the desert to the northeast. His was the Pintubi group that had been run off their land by British bomb testing. So he and they were but a minority in our camp. So he had a double effort to fit in with the others and with the whites. Since he had once met the Queen of England and made the national newspapers, he was sort of a spokesperson. The newspaper reporters had given him the nickname "Nosepeg," and he had taken on a kind of "Uncle Tom"-like turn in of the shoulders, a kind of soft-shoe shuffle; and he usually slouched and bobbed in an acquiescent kind of way. He had to relate to the whites more than leaders of other groups, and act in a way that secured his people things even though they were a small minority. He was working hard for his people, but it wasn't easy.

He wore an old man's coat. When I say this I mean this in a way that you might not understand. He like most of the others wore a single outfit for many months until it nearly dropped off. Day and night the same thing. Clothes were functional, not a matter of style and accumulation. He was friendly and confiding. He was uncertain. He needed allies. I liked him because he was friendly, in a way. The friendship was clouded by agendas, important ones for his people. He always walked as if he was in compromise somehow. I wished the world had not taken from him the power of the elders.

One morning there was a great banging on the door of our trailer. It was about five in the morning. I was not very awake as I rushed to answer the urgency of the knocking on the door. There he was totally altered. He stood magnificently straight, totally confident. "The ceremonies are starting and I need the keys to the car," he said. I handed them over asking nothing. I realized as he left that he had the magnificent bearing of a king, total beauty and confidence. He was wearing nothing.

It was a shocking contrast to his identity in clothes – something suppressed and small and subservient. In the space of ceremony, in his place of belonging, he was unparalleled. How had the early European settlers equated the naked human body with poverty and ignorance?

He Comes to Burn Me

One day I was sitting alone in the crazy tin Quonset hut that was the community office. It was hot sitting in the tin shed in the blazing desert sun. Ngunkumarra, the young girl who worked with me, had gone on walkabout. Her boyfriend had taken up with another girl, and she just needed to get out of town for a while. I had been alone, baking in the heat of the afternoon on a day that had lifted the thermometer to the top of its range (112 degrees Fahrenheit) at 10:40 am that morning.

It was a room with nothing in it but a single desk, a chair, a radio, and a small safe, all covered in layers and layers of red dust. It was hardly a method for representing civilization, but I and the office belongings were all the "civilization" that had been arranged for that place. Everyone was off doing something saner and cooler than just sitting in an office like I was. The daily radio contacts with Alice Springs, the other settlements and the flying doctor were finished. The mail, with its handful of child welfare checks, had been handed out. There was nothing much else to do, so I was just sitting there.

Suddenly bursting through the door came a young man, perhaps in his mid-twenties. He was wearing traditional costume – feathers and paint – and he was carrying all of his weapons. A spear was placed in his spear thrower, poised to throw with arm raised. A large club was in his other hand. He walked swiftly up to the desk, towering over me threateningly.

"I hate all white people" he said "I've come to burn this place down."

All this stopped my mind in its tracks. I simply sat and pondered what he had said. It felt as if my mind seemed to have frozen. He waited impatiently for me to respond, his hands ready to bring his weapons into action.

The truth of the matter was obvious.

"You're right," I said "It's yours. Burn it down".

The wind of anger passed out of him suddenly. He brought his hands and his weapons down with an out breath of air. The long term, unanswerable historical anguish still lay there between us. He turned on his heal and walked out into the red desert.

Consensus

"Can you relay the budget decision now? Over". The radiotelephone crackled as the voice of our boss from the Bureau of Aboriginal Affairs asked the question. The urgency and need to have an instant answer seem so real when he spoke it. He was a good man who spoke Pitanjarra and seemed to care deeply about his work. He was in Alice Springs and much closer to the demands of the busy world of Canberra. But we were not in his world.

" No", Ken replied, "It will be at least another day or two. Over."

"Call as soon as you have the answer. Over", he said with, an impatient tone that implied that we were somehow incapable in some way. We should be able to "make them" get to an answer sooner.

A *real* consensus requires real time if there is to be harmony and arrival at a decision that all can understand and feel. It was a huge gap between the realities of the community and the Bureau that it was our work to span. The meeting went on for another day and a half. All the while we felt squeezed by the Alice Spring's view that suggested there was something wrong with this effective way of making decisions. The urgency of time took on a greater precedence than making the effort to understand one another, which is the Aboriginals' way of proceeding.

I remember sitting at another meeting where, when one woman felt upset with the direction of the emerging decision, everyone stopped and turned to attend to how she felt before proceeding. The emotions and feeling alive in the group participants was not to be passed over as unimportant. It was not peripheral or something to be patronizing about or irritated with. It was real information to be attended to. What a relief to see and feel another way of relating. In their decision-making process no one spoke loudly and egotistically on their own behalf. The loudest voice was not the winner. The terms "primitive" or "pre-rational" just didn't fit here for me as descriptors of this way of arriving at decisions. We, in places far from that remote spot, are only now beginning to learn what real consensus might look and smell like.

Wirtu: Names and Death

I had to deal with names every day. I sat the old women down next to me in the Quonset hut and spoke to them in their language, so they gave me their Aboriginal names. They didn't give their most sacred name, but their daily name. I would write that down and use it in their files and forms to the government.

That caused me no end of havoc in my relations with the government. They had chosen or been given a "permanent" English name, like "Mary" or "Bill" or "Santa Claus," that Aboriginals used exclusively for whites and government things. I was messing up the cross cultural compromise when I tried to use their Aboriginal names.

Their names were not anything like we think of them in European cultures, or modern dominant Australian culture. The names they commonly used were not necessarily permanent ones. If someone died, all the people would change their name to another name (for example, all the Ngunkuwarras would change to Ngampitinja). If the person had died of old age peacefully, it was not so critical for everyone to change his or her name. If they had died young, people for a long way around would hear of it and change to a new name. The name of the person who had died was not mentioned again after they died. You could not say it out loud. In contrast to the ever-changing common name, the sacred names, though unchanging in a person's lifetime, could not be spoken. The whites around took this to be some sign of not being proper or civilized, but it was merely cultural convention.

Wirtu came into my life with a name and left without one. Weeks were marked by the arrival of the supply plane or an occasional flying doctor. Periodically government people just showed up on their rounds. The government piano tuner came one day (a day's journey from Uluru (Ayers Rock), but we had no piano. Government folk singers came through, accountants, school administrators, and lawyers. One of these wandering government people from Alice Springs came bringing a dog to give away. To me it looked like an old white dog. Having possessed a dog as a child, I couldn't stand the idea of this old dog being abandoned so I said I'd take it. It slept for two days, in a kind of exhaustion.

Then it woke up. Rested and fed it turned out to be a puppy of perhaps six months, with a beautiful spirit. There are some times when the cynical, random, meaningless facade of the world wears thin or has a hole and something magical can't be ignored. The dog, named Wirtu, was like that. His character was so noble, so somehow profound that he seemed to remind one that the world is indeed magical, a gift. Ken claimed that Wirtu had more personal character than he possessed, and I didn't disagree with him. His name meant "strong" because he was so well fed and healthy looking. The community had chosen his name. He lived for quite a few months with me until his death in a strange scene in a dry creek bed.

Wirtu expressed such joy in water that seemed so strange in that dry, dry landscape. One day we had taken my visiting mother Helen out to see a water hole just a few hours away. It was a special place, a huge pool of water surrounded by rock walls. It was a rare treasure out there, where even tiny pea green pools of sludge were a great treat to bathe in. Wirtu had gone on swimming endlessly even when the rest of us had finally tired and lay out to dry on the rocks. Wirtu had finally come out of the water an amazing bright white color. He returned to his usual dust red color by the end of the week.

The night Wirtu died I had taken my mother, Helen, out to enjoy the evening in a walk to a creek out near the Petermann Range. As we entered the creek area just as dusk was falling, Wirtu had become excited sniffing at something in the dry grass. Suddenly a huge green snake had rose and bit him just below the neck. It was a mythical scene with the snake rising to the height of his chest with fangs revealed. It was the snake that guarded the waterhole. I rushed to get Wirtu, not thinking of myself. As I grabbed the back of his collar the snake hit his neck again. I did not let go, but dragged him back.

The snake disappeared as I hauled my dog to higher ground. He slumped. I carried him back two miles in my arms. It was a long walk in the dark, and I could feel his body in pain. After our return to the trailer he was in agony all night, vomiting. I tried to make him comfortable, but at last he died in my arms. I had never felt the life force leave a living being before. One minute a living thing, the next an inanimate weight of flesh. Where did the spirit go?

There was something about that dog. It was as if he had come to instruct me in the nature of death. I wept. The next day an Aboriginal man who worked with Ken named Charlie came to see me. Seeing my sadness he said, "I'm sorry about what's his name". At first I was puzzled. He spoke with such kindness, but did not say my dog's name. Then in the next moment I realized that he had stretched the cultural boundaries as far as he could to soften my grief. "What's his name" was as close to saying the name of someone that had died as he could respectfully say.

Peter, the American mechanic, helped me bury my dog deep so the dingos wouldn't eat him. He had done it in a big hurry as if he didn't want to be around death too long, but it was a kind gesture none the less. Together we pulled a big old tree branch over the top of the grave. I always looked at that spot as I drove by that place. That dog had been so full of love. I thought a lot about how we come and then we go in the world. And how our name cannot hold anything.

Mad hatter's World

Warburton was a crazy place. Maybe the energy of the land was messed up by mining, or maybe it was just that way. All the white people who were sent out there seemed to go mad. There were four huge heaps of old cars sitting like monuments on the land near that settlement. It was said that they had been rounded up to clean the place for the Queen's visit some years before. They had rounded up all the old wrecks and made the young girls sing when she came.

Warburton was a settlement with a school, a shop and a few other random ramshackle buildings. Two sisters, missionaries, lived there too. Their work on recording the Pitanjarrra and Ngaanyatjarra languages was legend. Excellent work it was said. They seemed very sincere, but crazy. Everyone there seemed deranged.

An anthropologist friend of mine had worked there. Her work seemed good I suppose, but she had become lost among the strange wars of jealousy and paranoia among the whites out there, I thought. One of our bosses from the Bureau was sent out there. He too seemed to go through some kind of terror, redemption, and madness. After staying there once for one night, I always hurried through there as quickly as possible.

One time I traveled through alone in a small used car I had bought in Perth. Driving alone all the way back to Docker River seemed far and a bit lonely. I needed to get back before the rains. I drove into town late one afternoon wanting to fill up my tank and go on. No, they told me, it was Sunday and no gas was given on Sunday. If they gave me some, they said, then everybody else would want some too. This was on the

Reserve, so only locals would be the ones needing gas. I would have to stay overnight, I was told. I sat in my car for awhile feeling grumpy and wanting very much not to stay in that insane place.

I calculated the gas I had left in the reserve can and decided that, although it was a gamble, I might just make it without any gas from Warburton. I drove off into the growing dusk. The dirt road out to Warburton was pretty sketchy, crossing sand dunes where you just had to rev the car and hope you wouldn't get stuck. Beyond there, the track was even more faint. I came to a sign that said "Sacred Land No Entry". Not knowing that was the road that would take me home directly I respectfully went the longer route. As night fell so too did the first of the rain. It fell hard and continuously. If I stopped driving and gave the rain time to soak in, I might never get home that season at all, so deep and impassible would the mud be. I drove on through the night at high speed through the huge puddles of water on the road. The earth beneath was still firm.

Lightning began to shake the sky all around. I became exhausted, finally deciding to sleep in the car, even though it was the only metal in a vast flat landscape. Awakening in the morning I found the mud was getting deep. I drove on like a madwoman revving the car through the mud or taking detours out into the untracked roadsides, praying that my tires would not impale themselves on a mulga stake. Mulga wood is so hard when it is dead that it never seems to grow soft or decay.

I drove on and on like some kind of Mad Max driver. I finally reached a place where the puddle was undoubtedly axle deep and the side of the road too difficult to swerve up on to. I had met my match. I just stood there trying to decide what to do next. I was miles and miles from any place. My only option for getting a rescue might have been to light a bush fire, but the rain had soaked everything well.

After standing there awhile I heard a far off sound. It was a motor! Ken had concluded that I might be stuck and had set out on the rescue. They had set out in a four-wheel drive that had gotten stuck in the mud. They had returned on foot to get the truck. The truck had pulled the car out but had sunk itself, as had another car. One of the cars had carried on miraculously to where I sat. In it were Ken and the mechanic. I joined Ken in the four-wheel and the mechanic got into my little car. We drove on like Moses parting the Red Sea. My little car made it back to within a mile of camp before it sank. The little car and the truck had to wait for dry season to be rescued from those huge puddles that were more like lakes. I was glad to be home and not stuck in Warburton for the season. Docker had a sweet energy and a beauty to it. I was grateful to be home.

Multicultural events: Lamas, Elders and Rain

Friends in Alice Springs called one day to say that they were hosting the visit of a Tibetan lama (a Buddhist priest/teacher). I arranged to meet them at Ayers Rock to bring the lama out to see Docker River for a few days. I drove through the desert alone in the night. Driving fast I nearly ran right into a great white feral camel looming in the road. Luckily we both swerved opposite ways.

I found my friends, a gentle and attractive couple, camping with the young lama in a crowded campground full of trailers. It was a sort of shocking contrast to the Aboriginal settlement. People in the campground sat surrounded by a huge array of material objects, barbeques, and bags of charcoal, trailers, awning, cushions, generators, clotheslines, and motorbikes. I stepped out of my car and shook hands with the graceful young lama named Zazep Tulku.

The next morning found us visiting Uluru (Ayers Rock). Zazep Tulku chose not to climb it because it is sacred to the Aborigines. They themselves do not climb it, so he would not either. He chose instead to go around the backside of the rock from the tourist areas to a quiet place and carry out a *puja* (ceremony) for the earth inside a red cave. It felt right, sitting in the red cave quietly together.

When our visit to the Ayers Rock was complete I took him in the jeep out past the Olgas (the range in Pitjantjajarra is Kartajuta, or "many heads", which is what those granite domes resemble). He was young, probably about my age. And I had many questions. He knew a young, amazing nun I had met on the plane out of Perth enroute to Nepal. "How was she?" I asked. He only said, "It's hard to keep such vows when one begins so young, especially in the West".

As we neared Docker River in the jeep an old man standing near the road called to us to stop. He wanted to know who this Asian-looking man was. I said he was a marpantjara (shaman/wise man) from Tibet. We arrived on film night. Everyone liked and felt comfortable with Zazep Tulku right away. He talked with the old men and performed a ceremony for rainmaking, all things they could understand.

When he left I took him to the airstrip to accompany two girls to the hospital in Alice Springs; he earned his free ride helping sort out a big transportation confusion that occurred getting those girls to the hospital on the other end. He had that seamless love without borders that so many Tibetan lamas express, immediately recognizable without reference to nationality, livelihood, and identity. As he left I had shaken his hand while a man from Sri Lanka (who had come to train as the replacement for Ken's position as community manager) had bowed to the ground in respect and had been horrified to see me touch a monk.

Water into Water: Helen Visits

I drove to Alice Springs to meet my mother who was coming to visit. Helen was alone now: in her sixties, divorced and recently recovered from a serious operation. I wondered about whether the body tries to kill itself off from the inside if it does not want the circumstances it is in. I got a nice hotel room and flowers. I thought about how a mother's hands and cheeks are the first landscape that we know as a child.

Helen arrived direct from suburbia in Orinda, California. She had not seen any of the big cities of Australia. On the plane she had met a nice man who surveyed oil reserves in the Australian outback. He had amused her during the flight with tales of mining and descriptions of the land. I found her happy and excited at the runway door. We got a ride into town in the black limousine of the oilman. We spent one pleasant night together in Alice Springs talking and talking. That was to be her only taste of familiar civilization before the next day when I drove her straight out into the wild desert in the four-wheel drive.

On the way to Docker River we watched the passing beauty of Ayers Rock and the Olgas. *It was way out there*; no hotels, no buffers between the worlds. I was wondering if she would feel comfortable or succumb to culture shock. Arriving that night at the community after the long dusty drive, I showed Helen to the little room in the trailer that I had prepared for her. It was movie night that night, the one night each week when a movie was shown for the community against the side of a trailer. Everyone sat on the ground to watch it. It was pitch dark out in the moonless night. The desert was silent except for the odd scratchy voice on the soundtrack of the old movie. I took Helen out to have a quick peek at the scene. I figured she was tired from all the traveling and would want to go right to bed. Instead she was intrigued and immediately sat on the ground with everyone and asked to hold babies. She was accepted as part of the community within seconds, in stark contrast to so many of the white people who came out there to visit. Her heart saw them as equal, and the people's infallible intuition recognized it. Her preparation had been years of reading *National Geographic*. From suburbia to the tribal with almost no transition in between, she leapt the gap that whole centuries of Europeans had been unable to do. It was her keen eyes, too, that picked out the bitter school principal (also an American) lurking behind the crowd in some small building there, watching the movie, but being incapable or unwilling to sit with the crowd.

Each morning Helen went out early for a walk in the desert, just as she did each morning at home. Quickly, she realized that there were eyes watching and guarding her everywhere. When she got too close to the sacred ground where women can't go, an old man popped out of nowhere and without a word she understood that she was to go around. I asked her how she knew what he was saying when he had spoken no words. It was clear, she said. I have always felt that the telepathy or empathetic non-verbal communication out there in the desert is clear and can transcend all language barriers. Her spontaneous knowing of it confirmed that anew.

The way I would describe it later was that Helen just "fit in" right away; demonstrating that centuries of fear and hate can be released in a pure heart. Her arriving there was like pouring water into water.

Political Things

One night some of the older men, who were the lineage holders of a great sacred spot to the north, came and literally dragged Ken out of our trailer. He protested that he needed to eat dinner and rest, but they took him straightaway off into the desert to the sacred place. I remained at home sitting in the quiet meditation room. There were little shuffling noises outside to let me know I was watched over in Ken's absence.

When Ken returned several days later, he began to do what the old men had outlined for him to do. He contacted the governor of the Northern Territory and other selected government leaders to come to Docker River on a certain day to spend two days camping with the old men at the sacred spot. They wanted to communicate the essence of their relationship to these white men. Some people thought Ken had cooked this up himself, to politicize the Aboriginal community, but it had been their idea.

When the appointed time came, the political leaders were met at the plane and taken out into the desert. They had arrived looking puzzled, but intrigued. It was, after all, a strange but perhaps welcome escape from the office for all of them. Several days later they all returned with a glow in their faces. Something special had occurred; hopefully that experience would imbed deep in their memories as they went on as administrators deciding things about the Aboriginal lands. The old men had reached out to courageously share what was most sacred to them. They had counted on being able to reach the deepest level in the hearts of the government men they had invited. Although the government men had to head back into a world that would not understand, there was a hope that something within them had been altered in a way that mere talking could not accomplish. Even though it takes years to have the true integration of one's being with the landscape that the rituals outline, this drink from the river of the desert's spirit was intended to send a message.

It was an act of faith in spirit. Who has the courage in the light of the destruction of one's people, culture, and place to walk into the heart of the conqueror and speak, not; not knowing if one will ever be heard.

Rage

When we arrived at Docker we were told of a hospital
that had been destroyed down to the very last test tube.
It was a mere legend until the day I saw it. All the
rooms stood silent and filled with shattered glass. The
windows too were all shattered. It sat like a haunted
place out in the middle of nowhere. No one went there.
Somehow I could feel there was a reason for this that
made sense.

I had observed the community deal with some wild,
boisterous teenagers in a way that made me understand
the importance of empowering young males. I never
knew how the community had dealt with the young men
who had destroyed the hospital. The lingering
impression I had was that the whole episode might have
represented a community feeling - expressed through the
anger of the young men - about too many white people
coming in and imposing their structures on life and
landscape. In any case the ruined hospital stood there
collecting dust, cement walls with empty windows.

While I was at Docker River, three young men had been
acting very wild. They were throwing rocks and
destroying things with violence, just as others had
originally destroyed the hospital. I remember the day
the community "caught" them. They had been throwing
more rocks at what was left of the desolate hospital
building as a general outlet of youthful anger at the
world. The older men had taken them immediately off
to be initiated into manhood in long ceremonies in the
desert.

There they had been given responsibility as keepers of
sacred lore and landscape. They had returned as

honored men. Instead of calling the police and sending them to the jail in Alice Springs, to eat good food and watch TV and become bitter, they had been turned into men. To express their own legal system the community then held a court after their return. We all sat in a big circle on the ground. It was very formal. Each newly minted and now responsible young man was represented by an uncle, as a lawyer, to the community. Other elders acted as judges and witnesses. With girlfriends, cousins, and peers looking on, the young men felt embarrassed about destroying part of the community.

Surrounded by all those who had raised them, loved them, and honored them as men, they had to consider the consequences of their action,. Rage, anger, power and disempowerment are interconnected in this story. We have only barely rediscovered their notion of restorative justice and community witness here in the busy and ever more lonely "modern" world.

The Shadow Side: Internalized Violence

The community dealt with the alcohol problem by not allowing it. Young men returning with alcohol from Alice Springs were sent back into the bush to finish it before being allowed to stay in Docker River. Great, kind, caring men like Brian would look after their families and lives all year and then go for an annual two-week alcoholic binge in Alice Springs. Many white people in Alice thought the Aborigines were drunk all the time. They just couldn't recognize that the men in the camps down by the riverbed where not always the same men.

Only two or three times did I encounter drunken behavior at Docker during all that time that I was there. What came out when they were drunk? Every culture has a different way of being intoxicated. White Australia men seemed to get very violent. Our Aboriginal friends got sad, very sad. The women talked about the pain to the earth, the loss of sacred places and community. The men did too and a very few, but enough to think of it as a cultural statement, had killed their own fathers. Was it oedipal rage not released by other methods?

Then there were fights between spouses. These seemed like long battles and were accompanied by not infrequent wife beatings. It was depressing, but then it was outdoors with everyone watching. The white community out there simply hid it indoors where no one could see, and perhaps no neighbors or relatives could help or monitor the progression of a relationship. It is so easy to judge what goes on in someone else's community rather than reflect on one's own. No one out there came up with any prizes for perfect behavior. The basic flaws and complexities of being human get mixed with cultural oppression and loss of land and community. Amid the sadness and grief lie the gifts and tools for healing and reconciliation.

Walkabout

I remember one day we simply went walking. That day the mad frenzied energy and seemingly endless responsibilities at Docker River just seemed too much to handle. So Ken and I just started walking out into the desert, heading nowhere in particular. Other times we had gone to visit a water hole or a community or a special site, but this day we were going nowhere but away.

Within a few hundred yards from the settlement the land began to do its work. Seeing the soft sand, spinifex clumps, and mulga bushes my mind began to relax. In the sand the spinifex blades and the wind had conspired to draw delicate swirling lines as if they too were drawing their Dreamtime place in patterns in the sand. Indeed they were doing just that.

We just kept walking.

After a couple of hours we came upon an ancient couple walking back towards Docker River. Slender and strong, this couple could have been in their seventies. Their faces were aglow. Seeing us they burst into smiles. "You are walking the song line too!" they called out. They rejoiced at seeing us. They were returning from walking their lines and singing the songs recreating and re-harmonizing the world. Seeing us, more people doing the same thing, was a cause for rejoicing. They rejoiced that even the white people were out walking the lines.

They were out re-balancing themselves and re-balancing the world. When the balance returned, their hearts had become full and they were ready to return. They wore no more than a square foot of cloth between them and carried nothing but a bit of tobacco over their ears and matches in their pouches. The joy on their faces was contagious. They were going home full. They were going home to care for their people – children and grandchildren – and to tell the stories of the land and the lines again.

Never before or after had I been welcomed so deeply by fellow pilgrims on the path. Walking and walking the lines.

The Author's Story

How I came to be there

We arrived in Australia in 1976 with nothing much in hand but a dream. My husband, Ken, and I had come from New Zealand where I had been working at a ski resort, Mt Hutt. Just as we were preparing to leave, the New Zealand dollar crashed and we came away with very little in the form of money. We still had our ticket, a one way from California to Australia that we had bought nearly a year before. It had included all kinds of stops: Tahiti, Samoa, Fiji, New Zealand and finally Australia. Each place had offered a great learning.

I was a thin shy girl of twenty-two from Berkeley, California. I had set out to see the world thinking very simply: if we in the US are using up some ungodly percent of the world's resources I better get out there and see what the world really looks like. I had in hand a BA in Conservation of Natural Resources from UC Berkeley and many years of living, roaming and working in the Sierra Nevada Mountains. I needed to see what else there was in the world besides what I thought I knew. By the time we landed in Australia my mind had already been altered by living in the villages in Samoa. Already I saw that the world was not only what I had been taught to see. When it came time to set out into the Central Desert of Australia I was afraid. It was a huge cultural leap, especially for one so porous as I was.

We began our journey to the center by going to meet anthropologists who worked with the Aborigines. We met them in Canberra, Sydney, Melbourne, and Adelaide. The anthropologists seemed very bright and fascinating. It was clear that they loved the people they worked with, but they seemed strangely possessive of "their people." I wondered about this, suspecting that they hid a deeper connection under the cover of academic distance. By then I had begun reading every anthropological work on the Aborigines that I could get my hands on. The preparation for the journey to the origin of humanity had begun.

By the time we actually arrived in Perth, a city alone in half a continent, we had come to the end of our money. There was no going home from there. We did have a connection, though, a friend of Ken's named John. A graying hippie raised as a Shaker, John was committed to honesty and a search for pleasure. We took up residence in an extra room in his home, an old Fremantle Victorian house with wood floors and large windows.

Our first year was occupied with how to enter the center properly. Ken became a Tutor at Murdoch University in its first year of operation. Later I did too, working with Geoffrey Bolton, Australia's famous historian and teacher of the first class in the Environmental History of Australia. We eventually settled into an apartment by the beach in Cottesloe. It was a year of settling into place. A reddish earth, a sclerophelous bush, limestone bluffs. Slowly letting the environment sink into our bones. It was a time of artistic renaissance; Fremantle was flourishing. The beautiful old buildings from earlier layers of Perth's history were being renovated. Settling into the city life, making friends, and meeting contacts in Anthropology...slowly set the scene for the real agenda: to live out in the desert with the Aborigines.

Ken had led wilderness trips out into the canyons and desert of the Southwest of the US. Seeing the Anasazi ruins he had wondered what it would be like to live with people who still lived in desert lands connected to the earth". That thought had set our compass aim towards Australia, every move slowly leading us out into the heart of Australia. It was to be a return to glimpse "the original" hunting and gathering life close to the earth, spiritual life inseparable from red earth.

In preparing for the journey a year passed in Perth. We plunged in with the energy of youth: Ken teaching Sociology at Murdoch University and training himself in surveying and the Ngaanyatjarra language in preparation for his land rights work with the Aborigines; and I tutoring at Murdoch University and assisting a well-known botanist who was mapping the vegetation of Western Australia. It was also a year of learning about the forests and beaches of southwest Australia. We led hikes for the University, teaching people how to read maps, camp, and explore the Karri forests, the great white dunes, and the beautiful beaches. It was a year of exploring north and some areas inland, coming to know the forests and dry places, letting the beauty, sounds, smells, flowers, and bush sink in.

Inside I was still just a little jealous of my sacred place, the Sierra Nevada of California; nothing else could usurp my first love. But with time and intent the beauty of a new place could penetrate. The flatness of the landscape almost made me ill at first, but the beauty began to creep in. The stunning color of the birds, a beautiful green flock of parrots on a desolate red landscape, the endemic flowers, the shocking red in a dull green scrubland, the haunting beauty of the ghost gums. One day out in the bush of the southwest I had sat in the ticking red heat, covered with huge flies, staring at the "black boy plants," as they were called, and Jarrah trees, wondering if I could handle this strange place, when a kookaburra bird had perched next to me on a tree and called out its insane call "Ouuouuuahhhhouwahhhou". He seemed to be *taunting me. I was re-enacting that crazed edge of near insanity that the first European settlers faced. Could I really handle a place that was* this *different? I thought of the early European settlers and how they had to encounter this new landscape and how they had tried to separate themselves from it with things like patches of green lawn and the Emu-proof Fence.*

The Emu-proof Fence had been a shocking image. Ken and I had gone out in the bush to see a cave and returning we had to drive along the Emu-proof Fence. It was a dry year and the fence was supposed to keep the emus from migrating into the wheat fields. Hundreds of them were there at the fence standing in a daze of confusion. The road was on the side of the fence where they were, so we had to drive slowly along. Instead of simply moving out of the way of the vehicle, the emus had done absurd things: leaping headlong into the fence and strangling themselves, running ahead of the car and then leaping to their death against the radiator. Driving slowly and shooing them away from the car seemed to have little effect on their mass confusion and efforts at suicide. The fence was one of those monuments to the confused relationship to the land of the Europeans who came here.

My first connection with the Kangaroos was via death also. We had driven down to the southwest in a four-wheel drive. While we were driving slowly into a gas station in the early morning, a huge kangaroo jumped out of the bush onto the radiator, crushing it and killing herself. We had to wait two days for repairs. They always came from just inside the corner of your eye, most often when driving at sunset. Too often they would cross into the lane in front of the car as if trying to outrun it, only to achieve sudden death because the driver had no warning. The eyes of the kangaroos were very gentle: it was so much better to meet them face to face out in the bush than on the road. Their eyes spoke directly to you, the way coyotes do when they look over their shoulder before they run on.

Connecting with this land took time, but really connecting with the Aboriginal people would take even more. The turning point for me was a bicycle ride to the last whaling station in Australia in Pemberton. I rode down in summer heat with a small newly forming group of young people working to create an Earth First Group. We rode until nearly noon each day until the heat became unbearable, then we stopped to avoid the heat, eating greasy chips in restaurants by the road and holing up in campgrounds until early the next morning. As we proceeded south it became cooler and greener. On the last day in the cool of early morning, we were enjoying the sight of tree-covered hills when three of us, myself included, who were looking at the view riding side by side, suddenly crashed together. I flew over the handlebars and landed on my head. No helmets then. The others seemed okay, but I felt dizzy and delirious.

We rode into town, with me trailing slowly. After making sure the media noticed our arrival, we proceeded to a beachside campground. The next day the others all went off to roam the beach, a long stretch of white sand leading out to a rock bluff, but I, feeling slightly delirious, stayed all day in the tent reading a *book by Joan Macintyre, published by the Sierra Club, called 'Mind in the Waters'. All the research on the subtle consciousness of whales and dolphins compiled there deeply affected me. If animals were so profound, surely other humans were too. I needed to drop my fear. I decided then that I had the courage to make the cultural leap to live with the Aborigines. That night with candles we all sat up in honor of the whales killed and read aloud about how beautiful and intelligent they were.*

Back in Perth, at last I was internally prepared for the journey to the origin. The outer preparation was organized by Ken. He scouted everything and prepared the way for our arrival in Leonora, an old gold mining town half- way out between Perth and the very center of Australia. He was to become a Sacred Site Protection Officer for the Western Australian Museum. This job led him into the hands of the Aboriginal elders who trusted him enough to let him view their ceremonies and learn the location of some of the sacred sites. Recording them was one thing; getting actual protection under the law was more difficult. Ken took his job to heart, never writing about what he had learned should never be spoken, and only revealing enough to try to preserve the sites. Later even this became too hard of a spot to sit in with integrity.

So at last we headed out to Leonora. Some people had called it the "dead center," but to those who know the beauty of the desert these words make the heart sigh and open into the great profound peace of the dry earth and timeless spaces. We came to live on the red earth, in a small white house standing in a bare red square of earth. The neighbors waited to see us plant a lawn. We did not. Life out there was full of strange stories of the meeting of culture worlds.

The stories in this book are from that time, that world. Entering into the world of our Aboriginal friends permanently altered mine. I would never be the same again. All the stories here are true. If they alter your view, penetrate your mind, loosen your hold on a material view of the world even for one moment, then they will have been successful. These stories have lain in my heart all these years, asking over and over again to be shared. It seems to be my duty to not forget these stories, to tell them to you. These ordinary stories are stalking me and you, waiting to be heard. It is the Dreamtime, as real as your hands and feet, that is calling you.

Going out Further

At the end of that first year in the desert, I left for Nepal for two months. It was a break from life in the desert. When I landed in Perth returning from Nepal, Ken was there to pick me up, full of stories. I felt strange listening to it; everything people were doing out there in the desert communities seemed like madness, but my repulsion from it meant I was affected by it. Somehow returning from Nepal and the Tibetan monastery created such a contrast in my mind that it seemed unbearable. It was my destiny and gift, however, to head back out into the desert to learn more.
We piled everything we owned into a big truck. A man who wanted to work out with the Aboriginal people was with us. His name was John. He was a slender, reddish-haired hippie. He would accompany us out to Docker River. Everything was tied on the back of his big old truck: books, old stereo, boxes of files. Good-

bye Lorraine, Peter, Daisy, Snowy, friends, good-bye. Ken would not forget them; he would continue to work for their land rights for decades. He believed that fieldwork should be repaid with real contribution. I admired that and remembered it.

Our first stop was Laverton and beyond to Warburton, the madcap mission. The missionaries looked askance at us hippies in our truck of junk all covered with dust. On we went through the endless sand dunes. We had to collect enough speed between dunes to get up each dune to avoid sinking in the sand. It was blazing hot, well over 100 degrees F. I found I needed a wet cloth on my head to retain sanity in that heat. But flat tire after flat tire was a challenge to anyone's concept of sanity. Sitting in the blazing red landscape the material possessions seemed like a complete absurdity.

Finally we made it to Docker River. The staff was moving from trailers in a lovely tree covered spot to a new, totally barren location nearby, only because it was further away from the Aboriginal people. Our trailer was not ready so we camped out beside our dusty pile of junk. The other Europeans thought we were strange for doing that -- didn't we "need" the comforts of civilization, weren't we wanting to maintain "proper" distance from the Aborigine? After two days, our trailer was assembled and John helped us load the stuff.. Even he was amazed at how little concern we devoted to our material things. I took one empty room for a meditation room. John would join me to sit in meditation in there in the blasting heat each evening, sweat dripping down our faces. He left after awhile, and I saw him once more six months later out in the central reserve at an isolated windmill teaching people to grow lentils. The vast space and the isolation set off the simple myths of people's lives. People's stories can be reduced to a single metaphor, like the myth of Sisyphus. What was my myth? Woman-in-transformation in the face of alternative realities.

So, we were there at Docker River as Community Development workers. It was all-absorbing. I had never felt so "needed," and it was a twenty-four hour a day job. The first task after setting up house in the trailer and planting a few trees was to go to meet our bosses in Alice Springs. Our next and next above superiors in the Department of Aboriginal Affairs were fine, caring white men who both spoke Ngaanyatajarra fluently. We were fortunate to work with these two particular men in the vast ranks of odd people in this business. The first question they asked us was "Don't you want separate bank accounts?" Good Christians that they were, they wanted to be sure that we understood that this kind of work was murder on relationships. We kept our account together. Alice Springs had a vital air, not the languid decay of Kalgoorlie. I liked it. Returning via Ayers Rock I could see that it was indeed a sacred place. The Olgas, rounded stone outcrops, too, were beautiful.

Back out to the desert I settled into my job, consisting of walking every morning to the little Quonset hut, which was the community office, and being there all day. I handled the office work for the community and answered the radio telephone. I ordered supplies, diesel for the generator, and received the mail. I attended the daily radio contact with Alice Springs. I handled all government business: welfare checks, child support checks, and voter registration. Each of these duties was fraught with cross cultural significance. Most of the interactions were merely the madness of two totally different worldviews colliding. While the previous strange relationship of "doing research" was alleviated by now being in a more active and supportive role, there were many ironies and idiocies of being the interface between the Australian government and the Aboriginal communities. I longed sometimes to simply "be" in the desert on their terms instead.

There was a man from the community, Brian, who came to work with me everyday. He was always there to help hand out the mail, and deal with problems. He must have been about forty. We never talked much, but I liked his gentle and kind presence. I also asked for a girl to train. Skinny and pretty, Ngunkumarra came most days too. I trained her to file the records alphabetically to some extent and to speak on the radio, after the requisite English part was over, with the other Aboriginal communities. Some white folks considered this dangerous and said Ngaanyatjarra was not an official radio language. I yelled back one day, saying that it had been spoken here for at least 30,000 years. Some people may not have liked it, but nothing could stop us from using Ngaanyatjarra.

Ngunkmarra disappeared sometimes, once for a month. When she turned back up I asked where she had been. She replied that she had "gone walkabout" because her boyfriend had dumped her for somebody else. A great social outlet for pressure in human relations, I thought. An acceptable way of getting up and walking out when you needed to get space in your life, but didn't want to go forever. I often thought about the phrase "Only mad dogs and Englishmen work in the noon day sun" as I sweated out the summer weather in the little metal Quonset hut. I had always been one to prefer to go "walkabout."

Often people came in with problems for me to solve. I found that they most often came in twos. It finally dawned on me what was happening when two women came in on two successive days. The first day, one woman had hung back shyly while her sister had forthrightly stated the problem and what needed to be done to reactivate her government checks. The next day the woman who had spoken so strongly hung back shyly. It was her problem, while the other woman spoke strongly on her behalf. It was too egotistical and difficult for an Aboriginal person to state one's own case.

I proceeded to organize the office and tried to set things up so the community could do their own work, not "needing" white intermediaries as much. Ken, too, was working on this aspect of letting the community handle more of their own affairs. Ken believed that the Aboriginal people making their own decisions were more important than their making the "right" (in perspective of white cultural values) decision. This policy antagonized the white staff there .Ken had started a policy of letting the community members rent the vehicles when they needed them. This was heavy wear and tear on vehicles since so few understood how to drive or maintain them. But it was egalitarian and educational. The other whites hated us for encouraging this. Cars were to be kept for whites that could maintain them and make them last longer.

We caught a lot of flak from the other white staff people for all this. In retrospect, the opinion of the white staff certainly didn't matter. The storekeeper and his wife had fled to Queensland in a small airplane with thousands of dollars belonging to the community and were never caught. The school principal and his wife later worked at the store at Ayers Rock and had done the same thing (it was a common crime in Australia). The white staff seemed like gross caricatures of human nature. There was the mad, hysterical English nurse who had been there for years. She doled out antibiotics like candy and gave drugs that were banned elsewhere (Aboriginal communities seemed to be dumping grounds for this). But she was sustained by her love (if patronizing) for her Aboriginal friends, and she did respect and work with the traditional healer. So something out there sustained her. This was not true of the other staff members.

The store manager and his wife were Australian, from Melbourne, although he was originally from England. Why they were there I never really understood. It seemed that they wanted to escape the conventional life of the city and the pressures of business. It was shortly after we left Docker River that we heard the story that these two had fled with the community's profits. When the accountants had arrived to audit them, things had felt funny, but there was no way to put a finger on it. The school principal and his wife were an all-American couple from Kansas. Why they had come was unclear;, they had land and family at home. The man seemed to need a sense of power. I wished that there were TV so he could watch sports, or a football team so he could channel his hateful energy. The whites had no "cabin fever" skills, no ability to get along in small communities.

This principal never learned the language and couldn't relate to the Aborigines; worse, he envied those who could. This was probably why he hatched his plot of revenge, to move from classroom teaching to the store at Ayers Rock, where he refused to hire Aboriginal workers. And to finally abscond with thousands of dollars.

There was another couple, an Australian mechanic and his wife from the Bay Area of California. She was a pretty girl, doing whatever was right to be a good wife, but I couldn't believe that she and I had grown up in the same cultural environment. How had this woman completely missed the hippie era and women's liberation movement? The mechanic didn't understand the Aboriginal people well, but at least he was selflessly committed to teaching whoever wanted to know about mechanical repairs. Every Friday evening he grabbed the big road grader and graded roads for miles around. He did it in an angry way, like "Can't these lazy people grade their own roads and keep things neat and tidy?" but at least he knew how to channel his violent energy. This strange group of white people held up some kind of "norm" of "proper" behavior, which Ken and I were to be judged against. It was only later that they all showed their colors, Ken with his lifelong commitment to work for Aboriginal land rights and others with their thefts of community monies. What were my colors? This is another reason why I need to share the stories.

In contrast to these workaholic people, the "mad dogs and Englishmen," the Aboriginal people worked hard and continuously when there was something to do and did not work at all when there was not. They could work twelve and more hours when there was something that had to be done, or twenty-four hours for sacred ceremonies, but when there was nothing that had to be done. They did not just sit around in offices or at work stations. They came when they were needed.

The flip side of this in my work was that there was no private time in the sense I had experienced it in my culture. People came to our trailer to ask for help at all hours. I would feel overworked, thinking, "I'm in the office all day, why can't they come there?" But I had never felt so cared for, so appreciated, so fulfilled with worthwhile responsibilities, or so surrounded with community. So many stories were born by a knock on the door, accompanying the gentle feet entering "my office." Sometimes someone would come at night asking for a blanket if it was cold. I would say "But the store has blankets, can't you ask them?"…"They won't help us after hour.". I always gave them something

There was a pervasive and strange angry tension within the white community. For Ken and I there was an ongoing absorbing interest in the patterns of the Aboriginal community life. Ken felt fully absorbed in this life, but for me there was one thing that did not make me feel so absorbed: it was the role of women. Admittedly, in this work I had developed fewer close personal ties with women than I had in Leonora, since it was largely men with whom I interacted in the community. But the occasional wife beatings and the fact that women couldn't participate in the public and ritual sphere made me feel cut off. The white women offered no alternative for me. They were there smiling and appeasing the violent, pushy, aggressive energy of their husbands. The angry schoolteacher from Missouri actually spent his vacation going to Perth to find out something from our past to get Ken and I deported. None of the whites were happy that we had seen to it that the Aboriginal community registered to vote and voted. We were not maintaining the "proper" attitude towards the hegemony and correctness of European culture. That deep anger towards other cultures that the white community expressed must come from somewhere, some great fear of alternative realities of competing visions of land "ownership"... I could understand the cross-cultural confusions and insecurities, but why the hatred and anger? There had been white people my age in the Leonora area who had proudly reported that their grandfathers had handed out blankets gathered from small pox wards to the Aborigines, to kill them off. How could they live with that in their souls? And then there are people whose hearts are open, like my mother Helen.

Time out there seemed endless. The seasons were intense and beautiful in a place that was so connected to the earth. It had rained a great deal one night, a huge, deep torrent, a soaking rain. Suddenly the whole desert had bloomed, everywhere had become a vast carpet of intoxicating purple flowers.   It was unimaginably beautiful.   Ken sat writing a poem on his thirtieth birthday surrounded by that sea of purple. That night hundreds of huge insects, massive and strange, had come attracted to our kitchen light. The screen on the window had been packed with an amazing array of bugs. Perhaps they had all mated quickly that night, because they were never to be seen again once the rain dried, perhaps not for years until the next great rain. Perhaps the human heart is like this, waiting for a rainfall to awaken to the fullness of life. I know I am grateful for the rain of insight and kindness I received out there in the desert.
So this was the scene and the cast of characters for the stories in part two.

.

Going Home

Going wasn't easy. Just as a fruit ripens on a tree, the time had come to leave. The lessons learned out in the desert were emblazoned so deep they would never come off. Like a tattoo, or a scar from childhood, they were like storylines marked on my body. I could never see things as I had before. Never. It was too late now. The thin strange lines of dry reality I had been trained to see before, the linear view of history and human experience were busted wide open forever. I can sit and nod my head with you about various things that seem like agreed-upon cultural norms, but I am waiting for you... I am waiting for the holes in time and space, knowing that you will find them. Then we will talk about those places.

So I drove the little blue car back across the great Central Desert, me scraping the oil pan repeatedly over the dunes, while Ken followed in the four-wheel drive with whatever was left of our stuff. Slowly, slowly towards the soft salt smell of the ocean, with red dust in our hair. It was time to leave; but it was hard to leave.

I have spent years considering the level of integration I saw out there. You can see it was not idealized, but if I let dirt, old clothes and despair get in the way of seeing beyond material seeing, I would be a fool.

I would begin my Map Reading and Interpretation Classes at the University of Oregon with a class on alternative perceptions of mapping. I would hold up one small drawing of a sacred board. I mentioned the Song lines. My mouth is saying: "There are many different ways of perceiving reality. Other cultures have expressed it in different ways..." In my heart I am saying, "Look closely, I am showing you a door to other ways of seeing..." Everyone loved this lecture and was sad to move on, but would have been shocked if we spent all semester on this when we had so many modern scientific viewpoints to cover.

Years later Bob came to my class at Naropa University. I had heard there was an Aboriginal elder visiting town and I had invited him to the class. Bob walked in the room, an old man in blue jeans and a cowboy shirt and hat. His clothes were all worn and filled with the smoke of fire and cigarettes. The smell took me back to the desert. Bob is an elder and Dreamtime holder of the stories of Uluru (Ayers Rock.)

He sat down beside me, and with infinite kindness he leaned over and whispered in my ear, "And what is the subject of this class dear?" I whispered back, "We are speaking of sacred landscape and pilgrimage." He smiled and turned to the students as to his beloved. He burst into story. He told the stories of his place with his voice, with his hands, with his heart. Here in this class, after all these years, we were able at last to really teach about song lines, ley lines and sacred places without fear or ridicule The room became electric. After he finished we could barely speak, much less find the appropriate words to we wish him thanks. I felt unable to keep it together.

After he walked out, I declared a break in the class for fifteen minutes. The students looked a bit stunned. I bolted for the door looking for somewhere to go. I rushed to the door of the nearest office where I might find fellow faculty. I ran straight in on a small faculty meeting in the Core College office. I told them what I had heard and burst into tears. Caroline, Genevieve, and Loretta didn't miss a beat. They held me until I had finished crying. Then I apologized and wiped my eyes and to return to class. Somehow I thought I had to look like I had it together as a university professor.

When I returned, I found that a third of the students were also in tears, while half literally could not speak. No one had wanted him to leave, ever. They had heard him with their hearts. There really were no words to communicate the depth of his transmission. I asked the new, first year students if we should continue class, but my voice trailed off. "NO!" they said," We must spend the next hour just meditating in silence to hold all that he has said". They had not yet received any instruction in meditation. We sat in silence together.

Thus, I knew that the Dreamtime is alive and well and in our hearts.

Works Cited

Songlines, Bruce Chatwin, Pan Books Ltd, 1997

Voices of the First Day, Robert Lawlor, Inner Traditions, 1991.

Wisdom from the Earth: The Living Legacy of the Aboriginal Dreamtime, Anna Voight and Neville Drury, Shambala, 1998.

www.ingramcontent.com/pod-product-compliance
Lightning Source LLC
Chambersburg PA
CBHW022122280326
41933CB00007B/499